The Royal Court Theatre
Sherman Theatre Present

Killology

by Gary Owen

Killology was first performed at Sherman
Theatre, Cardiff on Friday 24 March 2017 and was
first performed at the Royal Court Jerwood Theatre
Upstairs, Sloane Square on Thursday 25 May 2017.

Killology
by Gary Owen

CAST (in alphabetical order)

Alan **Seán Gleeson**
Paul **Richard Mylan**
Davey **Sion Daniel Young**

Director **Rachel O'Riordan**
Designer **Gary McCann**
Lighting Designer **Kevin Treacy**
Composer and Sound Designer **Simon Slater**
Casting Director **Amy Ball**
Sound **Sam Jones**
Deputy Stage Manager **Charlotte Unwin**
Scenic Artist **Charlotte Neville**
Set Built by **Sherman Theatre Workshops**

Killology
by Gary Owen

Gary Owen (Writer)

For the Royal Court: **Violence & Son.**

For Sherman Theatre: **Iphigenia in Splott (National & UK/International tour), Love Steals Us From Loneliness (& National Theatre Wales), Amgen/Broken, A Christmas Carol.**

Other theatre includes: **We That Are Left, Mrs Reynolds & the Ruffian, Perfect Match (Watford Palace); Free Folk (Forest Forge); The Shadow of a Boy, Big Hopes (National); Crazy Gary's Mobile Disco (& Paines Plough), Ghost City (Sgript Cymru); In the Pipeline (& Òran Mór), The Drowned World (Paines Plough); Cancer Time (503); Sk8 (Theatre Royal, Plymouth); Blackthorn (Clwyd Theatr Cymru); Mary Twice (Bridgend Youth); Bulletproof (Replay, Belfast); La Ronde, Spring Awakening (Royal Welsh College of Music & Drama).**

Television includes: **Baker Boys (co-writer).**

Awards include: **Meyer Whitworth Award (The Shadow of a Boy); George Devine Award (The Shadow of a Boy); Fringe First Award (The Drowned World); Pearson Best Play Award (The Drowned World); UK Theatre Award for Best New Play (Iphigenia in Splott); James Tait Black Prize for Drama (Iphigenia in Splott).**

Gary is a Creative Associate at Watford Palace Theatre and an Associate Artist at Sherman Theatre.

Seán Gleeson (Alan)

For the Royal Court: **The Weir.**

Other theatre includes: **The Curious Incident of the Dog in the Night-Time (National/West End); Earthquakes in London (Headlong/National); The Contractor (Oxford Stage Company); In Celebration (Everyman, Chichester); Molly Sweeney (Bristol Old Vic); Aristocrats (Chichester).**

Television includes: **Midsomer Murders, The Café, Public Enemies, Casualty, Doctors, Dalziel & Pascoe, Burnside, Safe House, EastEnders, Underworld.**

Film includes: **The Last Witness, Cold Mountain, First Knight.**

Seán also directs for TV and film.

Sam Jones (Sound)

For Sherman Theatre: **The Weir (& Tobacco Factory), Home (Community Production), Iphigenia in Splott (National & UK/International tour), Hood (Sherman Youth Theatre), Arabian Nights, Heritage, Cynnau Tân.**

Other theatre includes: **Looking Through Glass**

(difficult|stage); **Light Waves Dark Skies (We Made This); The Sinners Club (& Gagglebabble/Theatr Clwyd), Blackbird (& These Two Imposters), St Nicholas, Sand (The Other Room); Blue, All That I Am (& Sherman), Ring Ring, Growth (Richard Burton Company, Royal Welsh College of Music & Drama); This Incredible Life (Canoe); Mordaith Anhygoel Madog (Arad Goch); Sexual Perversity in Chicago (Living Pictures Productions).**

Gary McCann (Designer)

Theatre includes: **The Girl in the Yellow Dress (Market, Johannesburg/Baxter, Cape Town/Stadtheater, Stockholm); 33 Variations (Volkstheater, Vienna); Three Days in May, Dangerous Corner, The Shawshank Redemption, La Cage Aux Folles, The Sound of Music (UK tour); The Pitmen Painters (National/West End/Broadway/UK tour).**

Opera includes: **Der Freischütz, Macbeth (Vienna State Opera); Die Fledermaus (Norwegian National Opera); La Traviata (Philadelphia Opera/Dallas Opera/Bucharest National Opera); Madam Butterfly, The Barber of Seville, La Voix Humaine, L'Heure Espagnole, Ariadne Auf Naxos (Nederlandse Reisopera); Faramondo (Brisbane Baroque); Les Illuminations (Aldeburgh Music); The Flying Dutchman (Ekaterinburg State Opera, Russia); Fidelio (Garsington Opera); Così Fan Tutte (Schönbrunn Palace, Vienna); The Golden Cockerel (Santa Fe Opera); La Clemenza di Tito (Opera de Lausanne).**

Richard Mylan (Paul)

Theatre includes: **The Believers, Things I Know to be True, Peep Show (Frantic Assembly); Starlight Express (West End); How I Helped Out Communism (Lowry); Crazy Gary's Mobile Disco (Paines Plough); Badfinger (Donmar).**

Television includes: **Marked, Byw Celwydd, Agatha Raisin, Waterloo Road, Casualty, Doctors, Grown Ups, My Family, Where The Heart Is, Belonging, No Angels, Coupling, Bad Girls, Wild West, Score, Doctors, A&E, The Bill, Border Café, Silent Witness.**

Film includes: **Don't Knock Twice, City Rats, Upside of Anger, Love Peace & Pancake, Checkout Girl, Snarl Up, Dead on Time, The Wisdom of Crocodiles, Speak Like a Child.**

Radio includes: **Look Who's Back, A Taste of Honey.**

Rachel O'Riordan (Director)

For Sherman Theatre: **The Weir (& Tobacco Factory), Bird (& Royal Exchange, Manchester), The Lion The Witch & The Wardrobe, A Doll's House, Iphigenia in Splott (National & UK/International tour), Romeo & Juliet, Arabian Nights.**

Other theatre includes: **Macbeth (& Tron), The**

Seafarer (& Lyric, Belfast), The Odd Couple
– Female Version, Moonlight & Magnolias,
Someone Who'll Watch Over Me, Twelfth Night
(Perth); Unfaithful (Traverse); The Absence
of Women (Tricycle); Hurricane (West End/
Off-Broadway); Everything Is Illuminated
(Hampstead); Miss Julie, Animal Farm
(Peter Hall Company/Theatre Royal, Bath);
Absolution (Guna Nua/First Irish Festival NY);
Much Ado About Nothing, The Glass Menagerie,
Merry Christmas Betty Ford (Lyric, Belfast); A
Christmas Carol, Gates of Gold, Grimm Tales
(Library, Manchester); Over the Bridge (Green
Shoot/Waterfront Hall, Belfast); Elizabeth –
Almost By Chance A Woman (Kabosh/Project);
Protestants (Soho); Arguments for Terrorism,
Cold Turkey at Nana's (Óran Mór).

Opera includes: NI5 (Northern Ireland Opera/MAC,
Belfast).

Awards include: Critic's Award for Theatre in
Scotland for Best Director (The Seafarer); First
Irish Theatre Festival Award for Best Director
(Absolution).

Rachel was formerly Artistic Director at Perth
Theatre. Rachel is the Artistic Director of
Sherman Theatre.

Simon Slater (Composer and Sound Designer)

For the Royal Court: Constellations (& West End/
Broadway/National tour).

For Sherman Theatre: The Weir (& Tobacco Factory),
Bird (& Royal Exchange, Manchester), A Doll's
House, Arabian Nights.

Other theatre includes: Amadeus (National); Carmen
Disruption (Almeida); The Winter's Tale, The
Broken Heart, 'Tis Pity She's A Whore (Globe);
Filthy Business, Wonderland, No Naughty Bits,
Enlightenment (Hampstead); Cannibals (Royal
Exchange, Manchester); My Mother Said I Never
Should (St James'); Ghosts (New Vic, Newcastle-
under-Lyme); Single Spies (Rose, Kingston); Nora
(Belgrade); Sand in the Sandwiches (National
tour); Untold Stories, Peter Pan, Pinocchio,
Arabian Nights, The Wind in the Willows,
Treasure Ireland, James & The Giant Peach;
Life X3, For Services Rendered (Watermill);
Deathwatch (Print Room); Fatherland (Gate);
Lady in the Van (Hull Truck); The Deep Blue
Sea, As You Like It, Death of a Salesman, The
Grouch (West Yorkshire Playhouse); Road Movie
(Library); Cling To Me Like Ivy (Birmingham Rep);
The Land of Our Fathers (503/West End); Two Men
Of Florence (Huntington, Boston MA); Romeo &
Juliet, The Taming Of The Shrew, Macbeth, Julius
Caesar, Henry V (RSC); Honour, Macbeth (&
Tour), Coyote On A Fence (West End); Lysistrata
(Arcola).

Television includes: Impact Earth, Dalziel & Pascoe,
Inquisition.

Radio includes: The Report, Honour, The Blood Libel,
Europe of the Mind, The Look of Life, 8 Days in
July.

Kevin Treacy (Lighting Designer)

For Sherman Theatre: The Weir (& Tobacco Factory),
Bird (& Royal Exchange, Manchester), The Lion
The Witch & The Wardrobe, Arabian Nights, A
Doll's House, Romeo & Juliet.

Other theatre includes: Chigger Foot Boys (Tara Arts);
Unfaithful (Traverse); Blithe Spirit, Macbeth
(Perth/Tron); The Shawshank Redemption
(Edinburgh Festival Fringe); The Seafarer
(& Perth), Love Billy (Lyric, Belfast); The
Government Inspector, Arrah-na-Pogue (Abbey,
Dublin); Twelfth Night (Playhouse, Nottingham);
Dancing Shoes: The George Best Story (Grand
Opera House, Belfast/tour); The Shawshank
Redemption (West End/Gaiety, Dublin).

Opera includes: Faramondo (London Handel
Festival); Iolanta (Operosa); Albert Herring
(Grange Festival); The Bear, The Flying
Dutchman, Tosca, L'Elisir d'Amore (NI Opera/
Opera Theatre Company); Agrippina (NI Opera/
Irish Youth Opera); Turn of the Screw (NI Opera/
Buxton Festival/Kolobov Novaya Theatre,
Moscow); Orpheus in the Underworld (NI
Opera/Scottish Opera); Macbeth (NI Opera/
Welsh National Opera); Stravinsky Tales:
Les Noces, Mavra, Renard, L'Enfant et Les
Sortileges, Orango (Philharmonia Orchestra,
Royal Festival Hall); Agrippina (Irish Youth
Opera); Die Fledermaus, Imeneo & Rodelinda
(Royal College of Music); Faramondo (Handel
Festspiele, Göttingen); Carmen, La Bohème,
Turn of the Screw, The Magic Flute (Nevill Holt);
Flavio, The Fairy Queen, Xerxes (English Touring
Opera); Certain Circles (Dartington); The Nose
(The Performance Corporation); Il Barbiere di
Siviglia, Don Giovanni, Rigoletto, Hänsel und
Gretel, Les Contes d'Hoffmann, Il Viaggio a
Reims, Pagliacci, The Medium, La Tragédie de
Carmen (& English Touring Opera), Suor Angelica
(Wexford Festival Opera); The Kiss, The Little
Magic Flute (& Wexford Festival Opera), Hansel
& Gretel, The Barber of Seville, Xerxes (Opera
Theatre Company).

Sion Daniel Young (Davey)

For Sherman Theatre: Llwyth (& Theatr Genedlaethol
Cymru).

Other theatre includes: The Curious Incident of the
Dog in the Night-Time (National/West End);
Mametz, The Radicalisation of Bradley Manning,
House of America (National Theatre Wales);
War Horse (National/West End); The Welsh Boy
(Theatre Royal, Bath).

Television includes: Hinterland, Our World War,
Casualty, Tissues & Issues, Gwaith Cartref.

Film includes: Another Me, Private Peaceful, Daisy
Chain.

Radio includes: Hoshiko, Inside Information, Dolls
Tea Set, Inside Information, Bisgits a Balaclafas.

THE ROYAL COURT THEATRE

The Royal Court Theatre is the writers' theatre. It is a leading force in world theatre for energetically cultivating writers – undiscovered, emerging and established.

Through the writers, the Royal Court is at the forefront of creating restless, alert, provocative theatre about now. We open our doors to the unheard voices and free thinkers that, through their writing, change our way of seeing.

Over 120,000 people visit the Royal Court in Sloane Square, London, each year and many thousands more see our work elsewhere through transfers to the West End and New York, UK and international tours, digital platforms, our residencies across London, and our site-specific work. Through all our work we strive to inspire audiences and influence future writers with radical thinking and provocative discussion.

The Royal Court's extensive development activity encompasses a diverse range of writers and artists and includes an ongoing programme of writers' attachments, readings, workshops and playwriting groups. Twenty years of the International Department's pioneering work around the world means the Royal Court has relationships with writers on every continent.

Within the past sixty years, John Osborne, Samuel Beckett, Arnold Wesker, Ann Jellicoe, Howard Brenton and David Hare have started their careers at the Court.

Many others including Caryl Churchill, Athol Fugard, Mark Ravenhill, Simon Stephens, debbie tucker green, Sarah Kane - and, more recently, Lucy Kirkwood, Nick Payne, Penelope Skinner and Alistair McDowall - have followed.

The Royal Court has produced many iconic plays from Laura Wade's **Posh** to Jez Butterworth's **Jerusalem** and Martin McDonagh's **Hangmen**.

Royal Court plays from every decade are now performed on stage and taught in classrooms and universities across the globe.

www.royalcourttheatre.com.

Supported using public funding by
**ARTS COUNCIL
ENGLAND**

3 Jun – 8 Jul

anatomy of a suicide

By **Alice Birch**
Directed by **Katie Mitchell**

Three generations of women.

For each, the chaos of what has come before brings with it a painful legacy.

ROYAL

Tickets from £12
royalcourttheatre.com

Sloane Square London, SW1W 8AS 🐦 royalcourt 📘 royalcourttheatre
⊖ Sloane Square ⇄ Victoria Station

COURT

ROYAL COURT SUPPORTERS

The Royal Court is a registered charity and not–for–profit company. We need to raise £1.7 million every year in addition to our core grant from the Arts Council and our ticket income to achieve what we do.

We have significant and longstanding relationships with many generous organisations and individuals who provide vital support. Royal Court supporters enable us to remain the writers' theatre, find stories from everywhere and create theatre for everyone.

We can't do it without you.

PUBLIC FUNDING

Arts Council England, London
British Council

TRUSTS & FOUNDATIONS

The Bryan Adams Charitable Trust
The Austin & Hope Pilkington Trust
Martin Bowley Charitable Trust
Gerald Chapman Fund
CHK Charities
The City Bridge Trust
The Clifford Chance Foundation
Cockayne - Grants for the Arts
The Ernest Cook Trust
Cowley Charitable Trust
The Dorset Foundation
The Eranda Rothschild Foundation
Lady Antonia Fraser for The Pinter Commission
Genesis Foundation
The Golden Bottle Trust
The Haberdashers' Company
The Paul Hamlyn Foundation
Roderick & Elizabeth Jack
Jerwood Charitable Foundation
Kirsh Foundation
The Mackintosh Foundation
The Andrew Lloyd Webber Foundation
The London Community Foundation
John Lyon's Charity
Clare McIntyre's Bursary

The Andrew W. Mellon Foundation
The Mercers' Company
The Portrack Charitable Trust
The David & Elaine Potter Foundation
The Richard Radcliffe Charitable Trust
Rose Foundation
Royal Victoria Hall Foundation
The Sackler Trust
The Sobell Foundation
John Thaw Foundation
The Garfield Weston Foundation
The Wolfson Foundation

CORPORATE SPONSORS

AlixPartners
Aqua Financial Solutions Ltd
Bloomberg
Cadogan Estates
Colbert
Edwardian Hotels, London
Fever-Tree
Gedye & Sons
Kirkland & Ellis International LLP
Kudos
MAC
Room One
Sister Pictures

BUSINESS MEMBERS

Auerbach & Steele Opticians
CNC – Communications & Network Consulting
Cream
Hugo Boss UK
Lansons
Left Bank Pictures
Rockspring Property Investment Managers
Tetragon Financial Group
Vanity Fair

For more information or to become a foundation or business supporter contact Camilla Start: camillastart@ royalcourttheatre.com /020 7565 5064.

ARTS COUNCIL ENGLAND

Supported using public funding by

"There are no spaces, no rooms in my opinion, with a greater legacy of fearlessness, truth and clarity than this space."
Simon Stephens, Playwright in Residence

The Royal Court invests in the future of the theatre, offering writers the support, time and resources to find their voices and tell their stories, asking the big questions and responding to the issues of the moment.

As a registered charity, the Royal Court relies on the generous support of individuals to seek out, develop and nurture new voices. Please join us in **Writing The Future** by donating today.

You can donate online at **royalcourttheatre.com/donate** or via our **donation box in the Bar & Kitchen.**

We can't do it without you.

To find out more about the different ways in which you can be involved, please contact Charlotte Cole on 020 7565 5049 or at charlottecole@royalcourttheatre.com

The English Stage Company at the Royal Court Theatre is a registered charity (No. 231242)

WRITING THE FUTURE

SHERMAN
THEATR • THEATRE

—

COMPELLING THEATRE FOR CARDIFF AND BEYOND

Sherman Theatre makes excellent work with eclectic appeal, champions Welsh artists, and promotes new Welsh work nationally and internationally.

We make and curate exciting theatre for audiences in Wales and beyond. We develop and nurture the work of Welsh and Wales based artists. We generate opportunities for the citizens of Cardiff to connect with theatre through relevant, inspiring and visionary engagement.

Sherman Theatre is a producing house in Wales, with a particular remit for the development and presentation of new writing. We also run a significant outreach and participation programme.

"SHERMAN THEATRE, WITH RACHEL O'RIORDAN AT THE HELM, IS A FORCE TO BE RECKONED WITH."

Exeunt, *A Doll's House*

 029 2064 6900
shermantheatre.co.uk

 @ShermanTheatre

 Cyngor Celfyddydau Cymru
Arts Council of Wales

 Supported by
The National Lottery®
through the Arts Council of Wales

 Cefnogwyd gan
Y Loteri Genedlaethol
trwy Gyngor Celfyddydau Cymru

 Paul Hamlyn Foundation

SHERMAN THEATRE STAFF LIST

Artistic Director Rachel O'Riordan
Executive Director Julia Barry

Head of Finance and
Administration Sally Shepherd
Head of Production and Planning Nick Allsop
Head of Marketing and
Communications Ed Newsome

Administrator Lauren Aldridge
Artistic Coordinator Sarah Jones
Associate Director Gethin Evans
Box Office Manager Liz Thomas
Communities & Engagement
Manager Andrew Sterry
Company Stage Manager Chris Peterson
Deputy House Manager Keira Wilkie
Café Bar Supervisor Robin Hannagan-Jones
Finance Assistant Julia Griffiths
Fundraising Manager Emma Tropman

House Manager Andrew Lovell
Marketing Officer Rebecca Price
Scenic Carpenter Mathew Thomas
Senior Electrician Rachel Mortimer
Sherman 5 Admin &
Marketing Assistant Siân Mile
Sherman 5 Coordinator Guy O'Donnell
Technical Stage Manager Stephen Blendell
Ticketing and Reception Assistants
Beshlie Thorp, Elena Thomas, Ellen
Thomas, Ethan Jenkins, Jack Law, Lizzie
Ryder-Smith, Lynwen Haf Roberts, Scott
Skelton, Tamar Williams
Wardrobe Manager Deryn Tudor
Youth and Community Associate Anna Poole
Creative Intern Nathan McCarthy

Thanks to our Café Bar team and
our Front of House volunteers.

BOARD OF TRUSTEES

David Stacey (Chair)
Rosamund Shelley (Vice Chair)
Nicholas Carlton
Paul Clayton
Rhiannon Davis
Nick Gibbs

Marlies Hoecherl
Keith Morgan
Richard Newton
Sian Powell
Marc Simcox
Owen Thomas

ARTIST DEVELOPMENT

We are dedicated to providing opportunities to develop and support new and emerging Welsh and Wales-based artists.

The sector can only continue to thrive and grow if creative talent is given the opportunity to benefit from the expertise of professionals in a supportive environment.

Our location in the centre of Cardiff, our position at the heart of Wales's artistic community and our links and connections with organisations across the UK mean that we are uniquely placed to nurture Welsh and Wales-based talent.

Our Artist Development schemes include:

JMK DIRECTORS GROUP

In partnership with the JMK Trust and funded by The Carne Trust our regional JMK Directors Group develops young / emerging directors and theatre makers through workshops, discussions and paid development opportunities.

NEW WELSH PLAYWRIGHTS PROGRAMME

Generously supported by The Carne Trust, 2016 saw 14 Welsh and Wales-based playwrights develop their craft under the leadership of award winning playwright Brad Birch.

For more information visit shermantheatre.co.uk/artist-development

❝ THE CARNE TRUST'S BASIC MISSION IS TO SUPPORT YOUNG TALENT IN THE PERFORMING ARTS, SPECIFICALLY MUSIC AND DRAMA. WE ARE THEREFORE DELIGHTED TO PARTNER WITH SHERMAN THEATRE IN FUNDING THESE TWO EXCITING NEW INITIATIVES, DESIGNED TO IDENTIFY, TEACH AND TRAIN ASPIRING DIRECTORS AND PLAYWRIGHTS OPERATING IN WALES, AND TO HELP THEM DEVELOP THEIR CAREER PROSPECTS IN THIS IMPORTANT FIELD.❞

Philip Carne

SUPPORT US

As a registered charity, Sherman Theatre relies on support from individuals, companies, trusts and foundations to help us deliver our work both on and off stage.

Support from people like you can help us to present a varied and diverse artistic programme, reach new audiences, engage with communities, and develop new writers and emerging artists. Every gift, big or small, can make a huge difference.

If you would like to learn how you can support our work please contact

 Emma Tropman
Fundraising Manager

029 2064 6976
emma.tropman@shermantheatre.co.uk

SHERMAN
THEATR • THEATRE

COMING SOON

LOVE, CARDIFF: CITY ROAD STORIES
A Community Production
13 – 15 Apr 2017

IPHIGENIA IN SPLOTT
By Gary Owen
Schaubühne, Berlin
6 – 7 Apr 2017

Brits Off Broadway, 59E59 Theatres, New York
9 May – 4 Jun 2017

Sherman Theatre, Royal Exchange Theatre
& Theatre by the Lake
HOW MY LIGHT IS SPENT
By Alan Harris
16 – 27 May 2017

THE CHERRY ORCHARD ⚡17
Anton Chekhov
A re-imagining by Gary Owen
Developed with the support of the National Theatre
13 – 28 Oct 2017

KILLOLOGY

Gary Owen

KILLOLOGY

OBERON BOOKS
LONDON

WWW.OBERONBOOKS.COM

First published in 2017 by Oberon Books Ltd
521 Caledonian Road, London N7 9RH
Tel: +44 (0) 20 7607 3637 / Fax: +44 (0) 20 7607 3629
e-mail: info@oberonbooks.com
www.oberonbooks.com

A catalogue record for this book is available from the British
Library.

PB ISBN: 9781786821683
E ISBN: 9781786821690

Cover design by Root

Printed, bound and converted by
CPI Group (UK) Ltd, Croydon, CR0 4YY.

Visit www.oberonbooks.com to read more about all our books
and to buy them. You will also find features, author interviews and
news of any author events, and you can sign up for e-newsletters
so that you're always first to hear about our new releases.

Thanks to / Diolch i – Vicky Featherstone, George Aza-Selinger, Hamish Pirie, Alex Hope, Keiron Self, Joseph Tweedale, Huw Blainey, Katya Hosking, Akira the Don & Patrick, and absolutely everyone at the Sherman and Royal Court Theatres.

The concerns about realistic recreations of violence that Paul voices in the play are largely taken from the book *On Killing* by Lt Col Dave Grossman.

for Rachel O'Riordan

ALAN

Gas leak? he goes. Any gas leak would've been reported to me. I've not heard a word.

I look at Mark, shake my head, Mark wanders off eyes already down to his phone.

No problem, I say. Show him the clipboard. Sign to say you wouldn't let us in?

I'm signing nothing pal.

Okay so I'll put down 'refused entry' – and I take a good look at his name badge – 'by James' and then we'll know. In case of any problems. Gas leaks can occasionally cause problems...

And I smile.

Alright, give's a sec, he says. Looks up a number on his screen, dials.

I hear it ring.

Ring ring

Ring ring

And

It goes to answerphone.

The doorman

Ends the call, doesn't leave a message. And – I smile.

The flat is a sight.

Like someone's spent thousands creating a beautiful living space with breath-taking views over the city and the river, then some other fucker's come along and emptied half a dozen wheelie bins of shite all over it.

I sniff the air and taking my lead a bit more than he needs to, so does Mark.

There's no leak here, I say.

Doorman says, what you can tell just like that?

Well can you smell gas? I say. I nod at a teetering tower of takeaway trays. Apart from this crap rotting down.

Right on cue, Mark pipes up: better fetch the sniffer, just to check.

Fair enough, I say. Waste of time, though. And I head out of the living area, into the hall.

I head to the front door, I open the front door – and then let it go. I do not cross the threshold. I let the door swing shut, me still on the inside. And as the door's swinging, I step into a toilet just beside the lounge.

I try to time it so I can close the toilet door same second the front door slams, so the noise of one will cover the other – but I don't move fast enough. And I have to leave the toilet door open just a crack.

In the lounge I hear Mark deploying what meagre chat he has. In my head I count out the trip I'm not taking, down to the van to fetch the sniffer. It would take me… so long to walk to the lift. So long for the lift to come. So long to go down seven floors. So long to walk out of the lobby. So long to get to the van. So long to fetch my keys out. Then the call would come. An emergency so I wouldn't mess around. I'd get off the phone quick and then ring up to Mark. I dial his number –

– and hear his phone go, just a few feet away from me.

He picks up: and I say nothing.

We practised with me really talking, but then there was always the chance I'd be overheard. So for this bit Mark has to talk to a silent phone. He's shit at it. Rushes, never leaves enough of a gap for the person he's supposed to be talking to, to actually say anything.

Ah okay, he says, gotcha. Right, on my way, okay, okey-dokey.

Okey fucking dokey?

I hear them coming down the hall. Mark telling the doorman there's a main cracked in the middle of town, we've got to drop everything get over there right now.

They pass right by. Only the toilet door between me and the guy and that not even properly closed, and surely he has to look and see me in here and then it's all over and

The front door opens. Four beeps as the doorman puts in the code. I hear him pull the door closed, and the bolts of the deadlock slide home. Their voices fade off down the corridor.

I'm in.

Now I just have to sit tight. And wait for the man I'm going to murder.

DAVEY
Dad'd fucked off.

You don't know, though.

Had he fucked off or'd Mum told him to? You don't know.

But you know Mum's there day-in day-out telling you off getting at you never fucking happy.

You know when Dad comes it's brilliant.

Off down the beach. Off for chips.

You come home you tell Mum she's just nodding, nodding, not a smile, nothing like.

Dad got me a cowboy hat, Dad got me ice-cream.

Did he, she says. You need a new coat, Dad get you that?

No he did not. Cos he never does.

And you never learn.

A bit after my eighth birthday, Dad rolls up in a red Escort van.

Always a different car every time I saw him, and always falling apart.

Got something to show you, he says. There in the back in a box, is Maisie. Just she's not called that yet.

She's nice, I say.

Mongrel, he goes, but mostly border collie.

Right, I say, cos that means fuck all to me.

You like her? he says.

I s'pose, I go.

That's lucky, he says. Cos she's yours.

And I look at her again. I reach out, stroke her head.
She turns and just gently – doesn't bite me, she just puts her teeth round my hand.

She's mine. A living thing. But mine.

Mum says, and we're gonna feed her how?

Dad says, I'll bring some tins.

And who's gonna walk her?

I say, I will. Mum goes, for the first two days maybe and then after that? And what about vets? What if she gets sick?

I've got Maisie in my arms, she's slobbering all over me.

Dad says, alright I'll take her back.

If that's what you want, I'll take her back.

Mum looks at him. At me.

Maisie's settling her face into the curve of my neck, and

That second I realise what the curve of my neck is for.

It's for Maisie to settle her face into.

I say –

Please Mum. Please.

12

And –

– Mum heads off into the kitchen starts smashing pans about.

I turn to him, I say thanks, thanks Dad.

I never called him dad. I hardly ever got the chance. And little as I was I could see, me saying it did something to him.

Calling him dad, made him my dad – more than he had been.

He says, I'm working up the coast. You could come stay. Dog'd love running long the beaches. Would you like that, Davey? Would you like to come and stay?

Smashing pans in the kitchen stops. Whole house holding its breath to hear what I say. I say

I'd love that, Dad. I'd love to stay with you.

He reaches out, lays his hand on the back of my head.

Course that was the last time I saw him.

ALAN looks at him.

That was the last time I saw him, for years.

PAUL
Here's an interesting factoid. Once you've come up with a product that earns tens of millions, you will find that you are deeply fascinating to a wide variety of people, in a way that you really weren't before.

In particular people are fascinated by exactly how an apparently unpromising idiot like you, came up with this thing that made so so much money.

They'll ask – when was the magic moment?

How exactly did the lightning strike?

They want it to be a lightning strike because – anybody can be struck by lightning. If it's a lightning strike then what's happened to you, could happen to them. And without any actual effort.

But it's not like a lightning strike.

What happens is a slow gathering of details that often seem unrelated and maybe not viable but they stick in your mind and –

It's more like a planet coming together out of dust, than a lightning strike. Except instead of gravity pulling the rock and dust together – it's you. With talent. And hard bloody work.

There's never the eureka moment of legend. There just isn't.

Except – with Killology, there was.

My twenty-third birthday.

I'm having the family round to my flat.

My first flat. Nothing like the sky palace I call home these days, but still

A flat. At twenty-three. For which I paid cash.

By no means too shoddy an achievement.

The tour is moving from kitchen to living room, but my dad hangs back.

He peers out the window, takes a sip of my by no means cheap wine, winces, swallows it like it's medicine. I say, there's some bitter if you'd prefer Dad.

He says, no, I'll take what I'm given.

It's no trouble, I say, pour that wine down the plughole if it displeases you.

He says, you know what?

I say, I do not Dad, but by all means, enlighten away.

And he looks round the place, makes sure I see he's taking it all in, everything I've done, he says –

– you know, you could've really made something of yourself. If you weren't such a bloody waster.

I say, cheers. What a sweet thought. And on my birthday –
how kind!

I gather us in the living room demand a group selfie and then
bring the party to a close, implying I have somewhere cooler
to go on to.

Family dismissed I jump on my bike, head to the office, and
wake the machines.

This point we were a tiny outfit, with just one legitimate
chart hit – a beat 'em up like hundreds of other beat 'em ups
available on every platform.

I bluetooth the family snap off my phone, lasso my dad's face,
map it onto the head of the big bad boss right at the end of the
game.

And I spend my birthday night on my own, virtually beating
the shit out of my dad.

Killing him horribly, then bringing him back to life to kill him
even more horribly next time.

Playing and replaying his death again and again.

And it is because of that night I become – everything I am
today.

DAVEY
She says Davey I gotta work the shifts I'm given or that's it.

Tea's done, microwave on full for one minute to warm up,

Bed by nine, yeah?

I'm moaning there's some Valentine's disco whatever at school
I wanted taking to.

Some girl I liked. What I would do with her if I got to the
disco I had no idea but still.

Mum's having none of it.

I say alright I'll just go on my own.

She says you can't, you're eight and a bloody half

I say if you're not here, you can't stop me…

She's no, please, don't do this. Don't do this to me Davey.

And I smile.

She's standing at the door, fretting about the bus,

The bus she's just about to miss and she's gotta get a move on but

Me, grinning, like I'm the king of the world.

Off you go Mum. Off you trot. I'll see you later.

And for once I'm in charge, she has to bloody listen and –

– like *that* face changes she goes in her bag says right

If I can't trust you I'll have to make sure,

And she gets out her keys.

We've got a lock up top that locks when you slam the door,

But then another in the middle we never use you need the key for.

You gonna lock me in?

Looks like I got to, she goes.

I say what if there's a fire, she says

She says – please just be a good boy.

Steps through the door, shuts it.

Locks me in.

And it's always like this.

I never go anywhere. School trips I stay home cos it's an extra five quid.

Never have friends over for tea cos we

Can't afford even two more sausages and –

– I run up to my room and I've had it.

This is it now. This is it.

Out my window the flat below've built a little lean-to

Around their back door. I'm thinking I can climb out

Crawl the roof of the lean-to, slide down onto their bins

And I'm away. I'm getting my treasures together in a Spar bag

And

Pad pad pad up the stairs.

Pad pad pad down the hall.

Maisie's nose bumps my bedroom door open.

Stands there, looking at me

Those big dark eyes.

She's not clambering down no lean-to.

And I'm ready to go.

Little bag round my wrist so I've got both hands free

And this dog just standing there –

– and so am I.

Not going, staying.

I'm stuck

I'm stuck cos of this fucking mongrel

I can't get away

I can't do anything

And I'm crying I get into bed

Trousers coat shoes everything

Pull the covers up, try to hide

Crying, crying cos I get it

This is it now

This is me.

I wake up, sweating cos I'm in bed fully dressed and cos

Maisie's climbed on the bed with me, I try

To push her off but she won't go

Keeps me stuck there.

I pull my clothes off, shove them out the bed,

Lie on my side, knees bent, to take up as little space as I can

And Maisie curls into a circle, huddles into the crook

Of my knees, her weight on the cover,

And if I try and move she half-whines, half-growls

So I'm stuck, neck and shoulder going numb but

Half way through the night it changes. I stop feeling

Stuck by the weight of her, I feel

Held.

And looking back

That lean-to would've smashed

The second I put my weight on it.

I'd've fallen, straight down to the concrete.

I'd've been dead, or broken bones at least

But for Maisie holding me.

The dark of night I slide out the bed for a wee and she lets me

Cos she knows I'm coming back.

I pad down the hall and

Mum's there, in her room. The door's open

Just a crack and I stop.

The shape of her under the duvet.

The same shape as me. Sleeping on her side,

Knees bent, but no one

Huddled up to her. I stop.

I look. I take it all in.

It's almost funny, she's this tiny thing

That makes such a misery of my life, and

Her room

Wardrobe cramped up against bed

Little TV she got for a fiver

And a fiver wasted cos it never worked

But could never bear to throw it away because

A fiver for Christ's sake, five fucking pounds and

On the little chest of drawers by her bedside

Can of hairspray, mug, the red strip

From the plastic wrap on a fag packet,

The radio she left playing all night, that tune

He hums a little of 'Lillibulero'.

You could pick her up one hand

Chuck her away.

And I take it all in and

– I'm eight and a half now maybe nine –

19

I think, look at you Mum,

All on your own.

And no wonder. No bloody wonder, you bitch.

And I head back to bed

Where I've got Maisie to cuddle me.

And cos I fixed it all in my mind, I've still got it now.

The view through the cracked-open door

Into Mum's room. I can still see her. I close my eyes

I could open them and be there again.

PAUL
Sitting there that night, despatching my dad in dozens of grisly ways, I realise something.

The core principle of all artistic production is 'don't bore us, get to the chorus' – and yet our one legitimate chart hit just did not get to the chorus. Sometimes not for *minutes*.

We made our players twiddle their knobs through all this tedious kicking and punching, when they just wanted to break necks and slit throats and see the blood pour out.

And in that lightning strikey, exception that proves the ruley moment, I conceived Killology.

A game that was not about the fight, but the kill.

And I got the idea from my dad. A birthday present.

Thanks, Daddy. Love, Your Son.

DAVEY
By the time I'm twelve I'm not getting kept in anymore.
I'm getting sent out.

Go out to play. Go on, get out, run about a bit.

Wear yourself out, you've been wearing me out all morning.

So out you go. And who is out there with you?

Other kids.

Bigger kids.

When you're twelve, a fifteen year old might's well have superpowers.

You can strain all your twelve-year-old muscles and a fifteen year old can pin both your hands with one of his, leaving his other hand free to fuck with you however he likes.

And fifteen year olds might have super-strength, but what they don't have is any trace of a conscience.

So Mum sends you out to play get a bit of fresh air, she's turning you out onto streets that are basically ruled by gangs of super-powered psychopaths.

The biggest psychopath on our streets was a kid called Eddie Randall.

Not big in size. Tiny fucker. What he lacked in stature he made up for in sadism. He would torment, hurt and humiliate and if you fought back he would say, I'm gonna tell my brothers you've been picking on me. And those words sealed your doom.

One time Eddie decided he was going to win the sprint, school sports day: and him almost a midget. Most of us did the decent thing. We let the fucker win.

But this one kid, Joseph – the teachers went on to him that he was a bit of an athlete. He'd be running for the county when he was older. Just teachers being encouraging. Good on them.

Except they encouraged Joseph so much he started to think that just cos he ran the fastest, he should win the race sportsday.

Against Eddie's explicit instructions.

So Joseph ran as fast as he could, covered a hundred metres in a handful of seconds. And likewise Eddie ran as fast as his short arse could carry him, made it over the finish line only a minute or two later. The rest of the class jogged on the spot around the start line to keep from overtaking Eddie, then wandered down the track once he was safely home.

Eddie was furious. When the teachers handed over the silver medal and told Eddie he'd done really really well *considering*, it just made him madder.

Next night a couple of Randalls grabbed Joseph in the park, hit his right foot with an iron bar over and over again till it broke in three places.

Said if he told, they'd do the left one as well.

This was an eleven-year-old boy.

He never ran again, and he never told his teachers or his mum or dad or anyone.

Eddie told, though. He made sure we all knew.

So one afternoon I'm walking home through the shitty park and I've already committed myself to a path when I realise Eddie Randall and his pals are setting fire to a bin directly along my route.

I stick earphones in, tuck head down and step quick as I can past them.

But Eddie darts across to intercept.

What, he says.

Weird thing happens when you're suddenly shit scared: your arse grips tight shut, but the muscle in your cock goes loose and you have to really clench not to piss yourself.

And I have to breathe deep as I take my earphones out, just to say What? back to him.

You think you're funny? I say something, you say it back? You taking the piss?

No, I go.

What's your problem, then? he goes.

No problem, I say.

What're you looking for then? I saw you looking at us. You saying we can't set a fire if we want to?

No, I say. I'm not saying anything.

Yeah you are, he says. You fucking are. I can see it. You're saying I'm a cunt.

And he's got me.

Cos I do think he's a cunt.

So

I hit him, hard as I can.

He plonks down on the path, puts his hands to his nose, as bloody snot drips through his fingers. Looks up at me, just not believing it.

Eddie's pals piss themselves. Everyone likes to see a nasty little shit get taken down a peg, specially the poor bastards who have to be his friends.

I stand over him, I spit down at him, I say,

You get your brothers onto me, and this is what happens, every time I see you, every time, for the rest of our lives. You see me, you get hurt. I'm always gonna be bigger than you, and I'll always be able to hurt you, and I'll never, never stop.

And then I walk away.

Put my earphones in.

Turn my music up.

Expecting him to come after me.

Expecting a stone whatever to hit me in the back.

Expecting anything but what actually happens.

Which is I make it out of the park untouched unharmed not even a word said against me.

That night I don't sleep till four Mum wakes me seven for school and I'm fucked.

Eddie's not in class next day.

Nor the day after that.

Nor the day after that.

Then it's the weekend.

Then it's Monday.

Eddie's in school – but says nothing. Doesn't even look my way. Tuesday's the same. I'm half letting myself just begin to think I might have got away and then –

Tuesday night.

Knock knock at the door.

Mum goes.

I hear some chat.

Creak creak on the stairs.

Door, opens.

Your friends've come for you, she says.

I don't move.

Off you go now.

Off you go out to play.

I say, I'm not feeling well.

She says, what. I say headache, cos it could be.

She says if you had a headache you'd hardly be staring at a screen.

I say I would, I'm stupid like that, you're always saying. Besides I've got homework.

She says if that's true then why aren't you doing it?

I say I was just about to start.

She says, has Maisie had her walk tonight?

She knows the answer so I don't bother to say anything.

I don't say – Mum, don't send me out there cos those bastards are going to kill me.

Because you can't tell your mum the streets are full of psychos and it's pure fluke you get home alive every night.

Because if you did – then she'd have to do something.

And what?

PAUL
To be fair, my dad had given me plenty long before that.

I remember when I was tiny him always saying to me, you can do anything, Paulie. You can do anything you want.

Once, I was about… seven? We went on holidays to some mountains and he woke me up after everyone's bedtime and we snuck out the cottage with flasks and torches, went into the woods to see if we could spy some badgers or owls or foxes or whatever.

We got to the top of a ridge. He said to me, what's the sky like, Paulie? And I said, it's – in the air? And he said, yes but, what do they tell you in school, that the sky's like, at night? I said, it's big? He said, yeah that's right, it's big – but what else? What else do they tell you the sky is like?

And I was getting worried now cos I kept getting it wrong and this would usually be when he kicked off and cos of the worry I couldn't think so I just said, I don't know Daddy, I don't know I'm so so sorry.

And he switched off his torch. The night swooped in on us. Dad said, what they tell you is, that the night sky is black. But is it really?

I looked up. There was no moon, no nothing. I said, yes Daddy, really really black.

He said, but is it though? You keep looking.

I kept looking into that black sky. And right in front of my eyes –

– the stars came out. The bright few to start with, but as I kept looking, more and more everywhere. And a thick band across the centre of the sky was dusted with points of diamond.

Dad said, how many stars are there Paulie?

I said I don't know Dad more than I can count.

And he said, they tell you the night sky is black, son – but are they right?

I shook my head no.

And he said no they are not. They tell you it's dark but the truth is there's more light than dark. And you want to know something even more amazing?

There is no dark. It's all light. There are stars everywhere, in every direction, in every spot of the sky. The bits of sky where it's dark, that's cos the stars are so far away, the light hasn't had time to find us yet. But it will. And one day the sky will be light, wherever you look.

I didn't really know what that meant. But it was, fucking amazing.

I said Daddy can we go to the stars?

He said no one has yet, little man.

But maybe you will.

Cos you can do anything. Always believe that.

And he gave me a big hug, and… I remember his hand, round mine as he led me down the hillside. I'd stumble but never fall because if I did trip getting past a branch or whatever, he'd just lift me up, float me back down.

And it stayed with me.

So when I was bored at the incredibly expensive school my dad sent me to, I'd just walk out. Go round a friend's place, sit for hours playing Sonic the Hedgehog.

Teachers would say what d'you think's gonna happen to you? What d'you think you're going to do with your life, if you don't get an education? And I'd just smile.

Cos I knew I could do anything.

DAVEY
There are a crowd of them. Eddie standing outside our door. And smiling. Makes him look near human.

For a second I let myself be taken in by it. He's come to apologise and be my friend. Bullies need standing up to and no one's ever stood up to him before and now I have, he's taken a long hard look at himself and wants to change his ways and will I show him how to be less of a cunt.

I know this is bollocks. But I take comfort in it, for a second. And that comfort is ripped away by the flash of absolute evil in his eyes as I step over the threshold.

Out of our house. Onto the street.

And of course the older Randalls lurking the far side of the road.

Maisie's bounding away towards the shitty park, nearly pulling the lead from my hands.

Nice to meet you, Mrs Davey's Mum says Eddie.

I give in, let Maisie drag me a step, then another, then another, then I'm walking, as if by my own free will. Eddie at my side, and his brothers cross the road, fall in behind us.

I look back and Mum's still there, sort of hanging half out the door, watching.

There's a look about her, like she knows she's a step short of some new idea, but it's just getting away from her.

I stare at her, I'm saying, come on, come out here in your slippered feet and grab me, they won't do a thing, you can still save me and

Not too late now, she calls down the street.

And that said

She disappears back inside.

Down the park, two more Randalls wait.

One them with some fucking ugly pit bull.

And the oldest Randall, who no one calls by his name. They just call him 'the Worst'. He's holding a long, heavy, rust red, blood red, iron bar.

And I feel my arse clench and the muscle at the root of my cock loosen, and my mouth is dry and

I want to say, okay, okay, you can just stop now lads, I can't handle this, I can't do this

And so I do

I do say those things.

The Randalls laugh.

The worst Randall says

We know. And that's what makes it so much fun.

And I cry.

The worst Randall says, yeah, go on, get it all out. We'll just wait.

I cry all the more, and Maisie starts whining, weaving the lead round my legs, worried there's something wrong with me, and I put my hand down to the back of her neck and –

For a second I stop sobbing.

For a second my voice steadies and I say, you're alright, you're fine, everything's alright girl.

For a second I am myself, cos I need to be, to comfort her.

The worst Randall sees it happen.

And the smile that takes over his face is a nightmare I never wake from.

He says, 'salright. There's no need to stress yourself. We're not gonna touch you.

We'll sort this all out.

We'll sort this – your dog, against mine.

And –

That's why they call him the Worst.

He finds the worst thing anyone could do to you,

And he does it.

Well? he says.

I look down into Maisie's black eyes and

I say

Alright.

PAUL
So with Killology it's all about the kill. Say you're executing a victim. You shoot him in the heart, quick and clean – gets you a point. But you shoot him in the guts, so he dies slowly – a hundred points! Or, tie a plastic bag over his head, then take a

hammer to his fingers and toes and turn them one by one into bloody pulp while he suffocates – for that, you get a thousand points. Plus it unlocks a slinky new move in your end of level victory dance.

People ask, how do you keep coming up with these sick, hilarious ways bumping off bad guys. And of course it's not us. It's the community. We released editors and modding tools with Killology 2 and these days, most new content originates from the players themselves. It was actually a player who came up with what most people think of as the signature of Killology – the golden shower mini-game.

For those of you that don't know it – you set up any standard slow kill. Say your victim is getting fed feet first into a mincing machine. To start the mini-game you hold your controller at dick level. On screen appears a stream of piss, yours, which you then direct into your victim's face. Obviously the victim is writhing from the unbelievable agony, but they'll writhe even more to dodge your piss, and the game is to keep your piss hitting their face as they die, and for max points their mouth and eyes.

Brilliant, gruesome, and bursting with the over-the-top black humour that our players love. Some kid in Mumbai made it. And now she gets a quarter of a per cent of net from every new Killology release. Sends her brothers and sisters to school with it.

DAVEY
In the end Maisie stops fighting back. She's just lying there whimpering while the bulldog rips bits out of her left hind leg.

The worst Randall says to me – I think that's done it, don't you.

I say yeah.

The worst Randall goes over to his dog, cracks it on the back of the neck with the iron bar.

It lets Maisie go.

I reach out my hand – and she lifts her head to meet it.

One of her eyes is gone but the other opens.

She looks up at me.

And in the dark of that eye, a tiny spark, as my hand finds its place on the back of her neck.

The worst Randall says: the kind thing, now, would be to kill the bitch.

I say, I can't.

He says, then I will.

If you ask.

Say to me, please kill my useless bitch of a dog.

I say, please, will you.

He says, say it like I told you.

I say, please kill my useless bitch of a dog.

And he leans over her. Flicks a knife blade out. Pulls the skin at the scruff of her neck. Harder than he needs to. Slices the skin open. Then digs the point into her spine.

She stops crying.

And when I say a stray came out of the woods and killed my dog, Mum calls the police.

The police come ask what happened. I say, a stray came out of the woods, and killed my dog.

They write that down, and they go away.

Mum says are you sure? Are you sure that's what it was?

I don't say anything.

But everyone knows.

School next day I have Mr Jones, Mr Black, and then break.

Eddie Randall comes up to me.

You gonna hit me then Davey?

You said I got my brothers onto you, you'd hurt me every time you laid eyes on me.

Well here I am.

Here I am Davey.

What have you fucking got for me?

Then Mrs Stroud and at the end Mrs Stroud says are you alright, Davey.

I say I am.

She says will you stay behind please, I'd like a word.

She says I heard what happened last night, that must've been very upsetting.

I pick up a chair and smash it in her face.

Cos Mrs Stroud had a heart of gold and I wasn't scared of her, at all.

PAUL
Ask my dad how he made his money, he'll say 'industry'.

That thing we used to have. Back in the seventies? 'Industry.' You remember.

Truth is, Dad worked in the office, of an oil refinery. If he ever wore a blue collar it was a fashion choice.

At the refinery, they had these massive reactors where all the refining happened. And every now and again they would need a clean. And you'd have to get in them. With all the chemicals and fumes and shit. None of the regular workers would do it, because it was incredibly dangerous.

So they hired what in those days they called a retard, and now we have nicer words for, specially to do that job.

They'd give the dumb fucker a mop and bucket, and send him where less challenged men sensibly feared to tread.

What a lovely thing industry was. What a pity we don't have it any more.

So one year, the sweet, harmless, affectionate sod climbs from the reactor with his lungs dripping out his nose.

It's happened before, no bother, they just find themselves a new retard for the next spring clean.

But this year, my dad's just been made union rep.

And he persuades the poor sod's parents that they should sue the company.

Cooler heads tell him this is the way things have always been done, and he'll end up on out on his arse if he stirs up trouble.

But my dad goes stirring anyway – because it's the *right thing to do*.

So they sue.

And they win thousands and thousands and thousands of pounds.

Next month my dad is laid off. Entirely unrelated to his union rep activities, you understand, just his post becomes redundant as the result of corporate restructuring.

But Dad uses his redundancy to set up a business cleaning out chemical reactors. Not by sending in blokes with bucket and mop, but with breathing apparatus and hazard suits.

Very safe, and very expensive.

But not as expensive as getting the arse sued off you if you do things the cheap and cheerful way, which is what all these companies now fear will happen, thanks to my dad.

And Dad's clean-up business, cleans up.

He becomes a millionaire servicing a market, that he has himself created. And I've asked my dad – Dad, when did you have the idea, to set up as an industrial cleaning lady? Was it after you selflessly helped this guy sue the company that fucked him?

Or was it before that?

And my dad smiles, and says – son, I got rich making the world a better place, and the working day, a little safer for the working man. And that's all that matters.

Carrying on his dad's smile, PAUL whistles a tune. ("Whistle While You Work")

ALAN
I come awake and wonder why I'm on a toilet floor.

And then I remember.

In the corridor I hear someone, just outside the front door. Whistling.

PAUL stops whistling.

Door opens. Alarm goes. Four beeps as he puts in the code. Tread in the hall. I hear – I feel – the creak of boards under shampooed carpet, inches from me.

And then he's past the toilet, into the kitchen.

I hear water going into a kettle. I get up

Deep breath. Deep breath.

And then I think of my boy, push open the door and march straight in.

ALAN
Alright?

PAUL
What the fuck?

ALAN
I just came to check the gas.

PAUL
How did you get in?

ALAN
There was a gas leak? You phoned?

PAUL
I didn't phone anybody.

ALAN
Aye well we didn't find anything so that might explain it.

PAUL
What are you doing with that spanner?

ALAN
Let me show you.
I expected the first hit would knock him straight out. But –
he stands, and wobbles –

PAUL
I don't think you're from the gas at all…

ALAN
And then faints.

PAUL
I come awake and – I'm tied up.
I'm tied up and he's – hunched over a laptop, typing – two
index fingers, not touch – and, given a side view, and a frown
of concentration, I realise –

ALAN
I catch an intake of breath. A whispered 'oh fuck'. I look
round at him.

PAUL
I know where I know him from. And I know just how much
trouble I'm in.

DAVEY

The next three years, I head down exactly the path you'd imagine if you saw me at twelve, smashing a chair over the head of the sweetest teacher in school. So at fifteen, I'm on the dual carriageway, riding a stupid seven-year-old's bike. Not really allowed to bike on the dual carriageway but then you're not really allowed to steal a bike off a seven year old, so what the fuck.

Then behind me, engine noise; I look, a big mummy daddy people carrier bouncing along, switching into the outside lane when they see me. They must be in some big mummy daddy hurry. So

I wait till they're just a few yards away and then swerve out in front of them.

Screech of brakes.

Then, sitting in front of them, I decide to see just how slow I can go and still keep my balance.

How slow can I go, how slow can I go...

The answer turns out to be – very very slow indeed.

Mummy daddy carrier slips into the inside lane, trying get past. No chance. I swerve too, and wobble along, their headlights casting my shadow massive along the tarmac and

There's just the tiniest hint of the revving of an engine from behind me. Cheeky bastards.

So I start to weave, from one side of the lane to the other, so it takes me even longer to make any forward progress but still completely stopping the mummy daddy people carrier getting past me.

And the mummy daddy people carrier toots its shitty little horn.

I find this to be pretty fucking unnecessary.

So I stop, right where I am.

Turn round.

And stare, right into their headlights –

– and the headlights snap off.

And in the sudden dark I see, this people carrier is under new management.

I don't know them, and I don't need to. Cos they are obvious cunts.

Only a couple of years older but out of my league.

One in the passenger side sprawled back, bottle in hand, feet up on the dash.

One in the driver's seat fag hanging from lip, and a big fucking grin all over his face.

And I'm a nasty little shit by now but this pair have me outclassed.

I turn, I push off the ground, I pedal hard and

I make a few yards on them while they're cranking into gear but they rev right up to my back wheel and I pedal for all I've got and pull away a bit, if I can just keep going another quarter of a mile there's a slip road and a street and parked cars I can weave between and get away and

Their bumper just glances my back wheel.

The bike gets wrenched out from under me, and I am surely going to die –

– but at that second I develop superhuman powers and fly, up and away

And then crash, very quickly, and very hard. My face is in a pothole. Mouth full of gravel, from where the surface of the asphalt has come loose thanks to poor council maintenance.

I spit the gravel out, and some of it is my teeth, from where they have come loose, thanks to the recent high speed face-road impact.

The people carrier is crouched over what's left of the stupid seven year old's bike. Back wheel's gone. The plastic diamonds laced into the spokes sparkle in the street lights. Really really pretty.

And then the people carrier creeps forward. Stupid seven year old's bike disappears into the dark under its bonnet with a crack and a shriek.

And the mummy daddy car growls through the gears and races right at me.

I make to scramble to my feet.

I get halfway up and fall straight back down again.

My nervous system reboots and says it has ten thousand new messages for me from my right foot, and they are all variations on fuck, fuck me, that hurts so fucking much.

I lift my leg off the tarmac and the thigh comes up, the knee comes up fine but then half way down the calf it just… sags and my heel bumps against the ground and I work some more superhero magic and transmute the pain into vomit which I spray out my mouth and I curl up on the tarmac to cry but

the mummy daddy car is coming to eat me up.

I've got to get off the road.

I've got to crawl to the kerb and drag behind me my snapped off foot.

And I say, how the fuck is this fair?

The world says, it's not. But if you want to live, that's the choice you've got.

I push off, from my good foot.

I twist and roll in the air.

Land on the leg that is not good at all.

The mummy daddy monster screams at me, and I scream back.

and then nothing.

Just the rumble of the mummy daddy car, idling.

The doors opening.

Feet on the tarmac.

I open my eyes.

The obvious cunts standing over me, smiling.

And everything I have learned about the world up till now tells me, the worst of my night is still to come.

They pull me across the road. Into the back of the mummy daddy car. My head come to rest in some kiddy seat with straps and padding and cartoons of puppy dogs.

They bring me to some flat or –

They play with me a while.

The way they play makes the minutes like lifetimes; and there are hours of them I have to get through.

But lifetimes later, they get bored. And they say –

Are you ready now, Davey?

Are you ready to die?

And I say –

ALAN
I came late to the funeral, slid into the last row.

Vicar had a black eye from falling off a stepladder and I thought, this is just another fucking Monday to you.

I never meant to go on afterwards but then I did, for want of anything better to do.

I saw his mum sitting at the bar, staring down into her drink.

I watched till she looked up.

She slid off the stool, pushed through people, threw her arms round my shoulders.

When it thinned out she didn't want to go back to her place and I definitely didn't want to start the trek back to mine.

We sat in the bar.

We kept on drinking.

We got a room. They gave us a discount.

We fell onto the bed and

I almost couldn't, but then I could.

The two of us, pissed and knowing we shouldn't.

Doing it anyway.

And Davey became something that happened to us.

A time in our lives.

And that's wrong.

Saw Carole a few more times after that. Always drinking, always slipping into bed.

I'd wake on my back, her on her side tucked into me, my arm round her, warm weight of her against me, her arms hugging mine into her breasts.

Once I half-opened my eyes and Carole's hair was dark henna red, like it used to be. And it smelled of smoke, like when she did. And the room was the room we made him in. And –

There.

There.

There he is, gurgling in his cot next door.

That gurgle he makes when he first wakes up.

The gurgle that will work its way into a whimper, then a sob.

I have to go to him.

But I know if I move, I'll break it, and he'll be gone.

So I lie there, eyes closed, hardly breathing.

Her next to me.

And him next door.

Feet away. So near.

And then –

– the gurgling becomes a whimper.

Becomes a sob.

Becomes a howl.

He's screaming out his terror and Daddy's arms will make it go.

But if I move I'll snap back to when we are now.

And I feel Carole stir.

I heard her say, Mummy's coming baby.

But if she goes then –

So I clamp my arm around her

Tight round her throat,

Just to keep her there,

Just to keep him with us a moment more

And she fights me off, she says

What the fuck?

And takes one step towards the door.

Towards the room

Where he isn't anymore.

And then she stops.

Because where was she going?

Who was she going to?

I say to her,

You heard him, didn't you?

You heard him too.

And I don't believe in

anything

but – that happened.

And you can never go back.

You never get to do that.

But we did.

We went back, to when he was still with us.

I don't know what that means.

It means, this world isn't what we think it is.

DAVEY
The view through the cracked open door.

I open my eyes I'm there again.

Mum looks so small she's this tiny thing.

I push the door open wide I go in

I cuddle up to her I say I'm sorry Mum,

I'm sorry.

ALAN
Some kind people knocked at Carole's door one evening.

They had time for her.

They listened.

They listened for a long while, and they came back the next night.

Carole started going to their meetings.

Carole found comfort there.

And now Carole's got Jesus, and Jesus gives her strength.

She stopped drinking with me, and sleeping with me.

And I'm never one to knock someone else's beliefs but –

And what did I find?

I found –

I found –

DAVEY
I start to wake with Maisie curled up on my feet.

ALAN
Oh Christ...

DAVEY
And even half-awake I know that can't be right.

ALAN
Oh thank God.

DAVEY
Because Maisie is gone, and I can never go back to when she was still with me.

You never get to do that.

So I know this must be a dream.

And I try to cling to it.

I try not to wake all the way up,

But still spark enough of my brain that I can

Feel her warm weight,

The sigh of her breath.

In my head I know I mustn't reach down to stroke her because if I do she'll be gone, but

My hand doesn't know any of that. My hand just reaches,

To find its place on her neck.

But I can't, it turns out.

I can't reach down because

My arms are trapped.

And the weight on my legs is not weight

It's pressure. It's sheets and blankets pulled tight.

I look down.

Some sort of little tent around my bad foot.

Bit of plastic pipe going to my arm.

Machines at my side, bleeping my heart rate, my breathing.

Really cute girl comes up, all in blue. Says to me, back in the land of the living, then. Feeling any pain?

I say no, not at all, I feel great.

She says, that'll be the morphine. There's more of it in your veins than blood right now.

You're a very lucky boy. Thank God

The police drove by when they did.

If those little shits'd got you into their car,

Christ knows the state you'd be in.

PAUL

Dad's sixtieth I take the whole family to Egypt. Resort to ourselves, trips out into the desert to see the Pyramids.

And I know Dad's always wanted to see them and always had the money just never known how to turn it into anything worthwhile.

He doesn't want to come. He says oh yes, the big man, whisking us all away.

But Mum puts her foot down, for once.

Out in the sand, we look at these stones piled up on top of one another. Dad says, imagine that.

Commanding these things be built and they are built, and your work stands thousands of years after you're gone.

He smiles at me.

Says, tell me again, what's that new game you're working on?

I say: it's not a new game. It's a campaign module for a massively multi-player online RPG.

He says, ah well. There we are then.

There we are.

And he turns away, from the wonder I have put before him.

And I explode.

And after I've been screaming at him for a good five minutes he slaps me in the face.

Not a punch. A slap, with an open palm.

He says you're so puffed up with yourself. All your success.

You were a success the day you were born to a rich man. That was handed you.

And you wasted it.

We're driving home and the jeep goes over. I break my wrist but I'm fine.

Dad is not fine.

When we pull him out of the wreck he screams.

He has seven different fractures in his ribs, collar bone, hip, and legs.

The local hospital they don't know what to do.

The give him pain relief but they haven't got the right stuff to operate.

But someone's going to have to operate soon or he's going to die.

I ask the doctor where we can take him where they have got the right stuff and the doctor says, home.

But then he says if we put my dad on a plane, that'll kill him. Something about the changes in pressure, his lungs are buggered and he can't take it.

So we're sitting in this ward with my dad under sedation and my mum sobbing.

I call the office to let them know I'm going to be no use to anyone for a little while.

And we just have to sit there and wait for Dad to die.

After twenty minutes the office call me back. People have been talking to other people and there is a way to get Dad home. The plane would have to fly much lower than normal, and burn loads more fuel. No commercial flight is going to do that. We'd need our own plane. Our own plane will cost a huge amount of money.

But I have, a huge amount of money.

I charter a jet, recruit a medical crew.

Calls are made, permissions are obtained – and we fly my dad home.

He's weeks in hospital and the recovery is agony and he's a terrible patient, but he gets better.

Journalists want to talk to him and eventually he gives in.

They say, without your son you'd've died in the desert.

He says, without my son I'd never've been in the desert.

The journalists laugh. My dad doesn't.

Later Dad asks how much it cost to get him home.

I mention a figure.

My dad says, that is an obscene sum.

I say, they told me there was no way in the world to save you.

That sum is how much it cost to make one.

Dad says, that is an obscene sum to waste on one man.

I say, what should I've done, leave you there?

He says, in the old days, we had something called solidarity. I bet you can't tell me what that means.

I say I could try, but I bet I get it wrong.

He says, it meant, we stood together, and held each other's hands against the dark.

And when you waste that obscene sum saving me

You take the fucking piss, son.

You take the piss out of everyone who loses their loved ones for want of money.

You take the piss out of their grief.

I say

Don't mention it, Dad.

Any time.

ALAN
I found a community.

Communities really. Online.

Complete strangers, sharing the darkest moments of their lives and finding

Complete strangers reaching out to them.

There were forums for people who had lost – anyone.

Then within those, sub-forums, dedicated to those who'd lost

Parents, partners,

Children.

And then within those, sub-forums for those who had lost

Their children to sickness.

Their children to accident.

Their children to suicide.

Their children to murder.

And within that

Mostly threads of family destruction but then

Murders in which the perpetrators had been

Watching certain kinds of films, playing certain kinds of games

Devouring extreme videos in the murky corners of the internet and

The wounded families wonder, did this dark stuff have an effect?

And then I find

Deep in archived pages, threads going back years

A long series of posts in which a bereaved dad writes about

The American Civil War. Of all things.

And he's on about the rifles they used. These old-fashioned rifles where you put the powder down the barrel, and the shot on top of that.

And when they dug up the battle grounds, they found loads of rifles where the barrels were full. They'd been loaded, and loaded and loaded again, shot on top of shot, powder on top of powder, and never fired.

The soldiers would load their gun, raise to their shoulder, pretend to fire – but not. And with all the noise and commotion no one could tell they weren't really shooting.

But why?

The other side were shooting at them so –

Why did they not defend themselves?

Because there is an instinctive revulsion against taking a human life.

And that revulsion lives in our hearts

And that revulsion is the best part of us.

And that revulsion can be conquered.

PAUL
Yes, Killology is controversial. Breaking boundaries always is, and the establishment always forecasts disaster to defend its privilege. Free the slaves? Waah, the economy will collapse. Economy's still going. Votes for women? But they'll vote – for women! Well, evidently they don't. Let the gays marry? – God will smite us down! And yet – all this wedded bumsex, and unsmited we remain.

Let ordinary people play a game they love, bought with money they earned, in what little time they have for themselves?

No fucking *way*.

Of course, if the snowflakes had the wit or integrity to actually even play the game, they would see Killology is a deeply moral experience. It forces you to confront the consequences of your actions. Most games, you shoot somebody, they die, you shoot the next one. In Killology, as you torture your victim, they will beg, plead, and bleed and you watch the reality of their suffering.

You have to. If you look away the sensor picks it up and deducts points.

ALAN
He writes about armies. About how they make men into soldiers. About how they've developed a whole science of getting over that instinctive revulsion at killing.

And now with each new war, more and more soldiers are actually trying to kill each other.

And how come?

Practise.

Practise that is as close as it can be to the real thing.

So instead of shooting a straw target at the end of a field,

They run through buildings with smoke and explosions and screaming and other soldiers shooting back at them.

They practise the action of killing time after time after time.

And though they know the practise isn't real,

Rehearsal teaches the body what to do

Makes it possible for the body to act

Even while the mind is paralysed, by revulsion.

PAUL

And people say, but Paul. Mr Thompson. *Paulie.*

Doesn't your game put ideas in people's heads?

Specifically, does it not put the idea in people's heads, that it might be a super-fun thing to go around torturing other people to death?

And I say –

It's a game.

And when people are playing a game, they know they're playing a game.

If people play a game in which they are wizards and can command pigs to fly it doesn't make them believe that pigs can be commanded to fly in real life, because people are not morons.

And if you genuinely don't know the difference between a game and reality, then you are batshit fucking insane and it's not our game that makes you a danger to the public, it's your being batshit fucking insane.

ALAN

I printed it all out. Followed up the references. Books and papers on

How soldiers these days are trained in ever more realistic exercises.

And these exercises get the soldiers over their fear of killing

Even though the soldiers know they're fake.

Because it's not about what you know in your head.

It's about what you feel in your gut.

It's about responses your nerves learn

That completely by-pass the brain.

And that's what these games do.

They train our kids to kill.

I reach out to others in the community

With what I've learned. Most people

Think I'm nuts, broken by my grief.

But one dad gets back to me.

His name is Mark.

He messages and says

We have to stop them.

What's your plan?

PAUL
And from time to time some well-fed public official in some pussy country like Canada or New Zealand will announce she's going to ban our game and I say –

Go right ahead.

Because a ban from some soon to be bankrupt government is the sort of publicity it takes millions of dollars for us to buy.

Meanwhile all the kids you're trying to protect from our silly little game will download it illegally, without paying us, without paying tax towards your crumbling infrastructure. Excellent work there, government lady.

ALAN
You back with us?
You fainted. You keep doing that.

PAUL
Please let me go.

ALAN
I will, of course.

PAUL
You will?

ALAN
Of course.
But first we need to talk.

PAUL
If it's money –

ALAN
It's not.

PAUL
I did want to – some kind of offer maybe but

I didn't want to – seem to be insulting.

ALAN
You know who I am?

PAUL nods.

ALAN
Who am I?

PAUL doesn't answer.

ALAN
I'm that kid's dad.
That's right.
Can't remember his name though.

PAUL
I would, of course, normally, but –
– panicking a bit to be honest.

ALAN
Well I didn't want to do this.
We did email you.

PAUL
I get a lot of email.

ALAN
No, course.

PAUL
So I'm sorry if I didn't read yours.

ALAN
You did.

PAUL
I did?

ALAN
You said you did.
When you replied.

PAUL
Right, yeah…

ALAN
You said you were
Terribly, terribly sorry
For what had happened to my son
But you had examined the issues
And looked into your heart
And you honestly did not feel
You were in any way responsible.

PAUL
Okay.

ALAN
And you're right.
Course you are.
It's the fuckers who did the thing
That did the thing.

PAUL
And I believe the police caught them?

ALAN
Yes they did.

PAUL
Thank God for that. At least.

ALAN
But the thing is…

PAUL
What?

ALAN
It was them.
But it was you too.
Which is why I've come here tonight.

PAUL
To get revenge.

ALAN
To get you to stop.

PAUL
To stop?
Stop making games?

ALAN
Stop making, you know,
Nasty games.

PAUL
I should make… nice games?

ALAN
Could you do that? If you had to.

PAUL
Sonic the Hedgehog sells millions.
Mario Bros – that's just Italian plumbers, nothing nasty there.

ALAN
So you could?

PAUL
But other people will make nasty games.

ALAN
For now let's keep this
To me, and you.

PAUL
Okay.

ALAN
Okay?

PAUL
I'll stop making nasty games.

ALAN
You will?

PAUL
Yes, yes alright.

ALAN considers.

ALAN
Thing is.
You would say that now though, wouldn't you.

PAUL
Yeah.

ALAN
I think with you all tied up and helpless, you'll say
Whatever I want to hear.
So how can I believe a word that comes out of your mouth?
Given the situation.

PAUL
Well, this is the situation we're in, and, not wanting to be a
dick about it, we're in this situation mainly thanks to you.

ALAN
I suppose that's true.

PAUL
You could untie me, and then leave, and go downstairs, and out of the building, and away, and tomorrow I'll look through your email again and have a proper think about it.

ALAN
No I don't think I'm going to do that.

PAUL
No I didn't think you would.

ALAN
We emailed you before, loads of facts and documents, and it made no difference. But now – I'm supposed to believe you've changed your mind?

PAUL
I suppose it's not what you're saying, so much as the way you're saying it.

ALAN
Right.

PAUL
Having broken into my house
And hit me and tied me up, that's all given
Your words a new weight.

ALAN
Uh-huh.

PAUL
And I can see
What has happened to you.
And seeing that it makes me think
Like probably I think nothing I've done is anything to do
With what happened to your kid?
But seeing you
– I don't even want to take the risk
That I'm in any way responsible for that.
You get me?
That's what's different, now.

You.
Looking you in the eye.
Man to man.
Seeing your –
This had been a life-changing experience for me, I swear.

They look at each other.

PAUL
Okay, okay. We've used horror and gore and shock cos it's easy, cos it's easier to be extreme than to be really fucking good, and that was lazy, and stupid, and evil, and we're stopping doing it now. Okay? From now on, we do the hard thing. We just make really good games. Because Jesus Christ I don't want to be part of whatever the fuck has done this to you.

ALAN
Okay alright.

PAUL
You believe me?

ALAN
I believe you mean it.

PAUL
I swear I fucking do.

ALAN
I believe you mean it… right now.
But. The thing is.

ALAN begins getting items from his tool bag, laying them out for PAUL to see.

A chisel. A hammer. A tenon saw.

ALAN
I don't know if you'll recognise these implements.

A small blow torch.

PAUL
Listen. Listen.

ALAN
These are the items a player must collect and use
In order to complete Level 9 of your game
With the highest possible score.

PAUL
When I got home.
I could tell there'd been a break-in. I typed a code on my alarm
It's called a duress code, it tells
The security company I'm being held hostage
And the police will be here, any time now –

ALAN
I didn't break in. I was admitted.

PAUL
This is the rest of your life, locked up.
Think about what you're doing.
You can't get away with this.

ALAN
I know.

PAUL
You know?

ALAN
D'you think I'm stupid, Paul?

PAUL
No.

ALAN
D'you think I'm mad?

PAUL
Fucking obviously *yes.*

    ALAN considers.

ALAN
Fair comment.

When they tried the kids who… abducted

My son, it was quick.

Not quick, but not months.

There was never really any doubt because

They'd videoed it on their phones.

You could see the faces.

You could see who did what.

You could see whose idea it was, to play out the scene from the game.

And they didn't have all the things they needed.

They had to improvise.

Bread knife for the saw.

Lighter instead of a blow torch.

And you can see – Davey knows the game too.

He knows what's coming, and –

When it came to showing the video in court

I couldn't go in.

I said I didn't want to make what happened more real,
by actually seeing it happen.

And I did feel that. Though I knew it was bollocks.

Really it was that the kids.

The kids spent most of the trial giggling to their mates in the gallery.

I'd watch them.

If they looked at me I'd look away cos on the first day one of them

Met my eye and –

If I'd seen them laugh at the tape of my boy screaming, it would've been the end of me.

I don't mean, I'd've gone nuts and killed them with my bare hands.

I mean something else.

But then after the trial, I started to think

If my boy lived through that, don't I have to watch it?

Like, if I didn't watch it, I was leaving him to go through it alone?

And that was obviously bullshit.

But hard to shake off all the same.

ALAN turns back to PAUL.

ALAN
What we're going to do is

We'll watch what happened to my son,

Together. The two of us.

And then I'll use that as a guide.

For what I'm going to do to you.

It'll just take sec for the disc to load.

So this is it now.

The audience don't see what plays. Just hear.

ALAN notices PAUL isn't watching.

ALAN
Don't you dare look away.

PAUL still not watching.

ALAN
Watch it.

PAUL
No.

ALAN
Fucking watch it. Watch it you cunt.

PAUL
Or you'll what?

ALAN says nothing.

PAUL
I didn't do it. I'm not watching it.

ALAN
Watch it. Please.

PAUL
No.

ALAN gathers himself.

ALAN
Alright then, you'll see soon enough.

From the video, a tap of metal on metal, and the pleading voice becomes a scream, the other boys cheering, whooping, swearing in disbelief and horror as the blows continue.

ALAN watches say twenty or thirty seconds of the footage of his son being tortured, not aware of PAUL now.

He goes to the laptop, stops the video.

Takes some time to collect himself.

PAUL
And you're going to do that, are you?

ALAN
Right.

PAUL
You're going to do that, to me?

ALAN
Right then.

> *ALAN picks up the hammer and chisel. Puts the blade of the chisel to PAUL's abdomen.*

ALAN
Okey-fucking-dokey.

> *PAUL pleads with him.*

> *ALAN psychs himself to bring the hammer down on the chisel's handle.*

> *A couple of practise swings, like a golfer. Little taps of metal on metal as the hammer makes contact with the chisel.*

> *And then ALAN brings the hammer down hard –*

> *– PAUL screams –*

> *But ALAN has stopped his swing short of the chisel.*

> *He puts down the hammer and chisel.*

[INTERVAL]

DAVEY

After a few weeks in hospital a woman called Jill comes to torture me into walking.

I say, I can't, it hurts, what're you some kind of sadist?

She says yes, that's exactly right. It was this or serial killing, and serial killers don't get maternity. So I chose physio.

As I get so's I can walk with a frame I start to explore. I leave my ward, my corridor – I make it as far as the lift and

The place is massive.

It's got its own shops.

Soon I'm good at getting around with the frame, so my physio-sadist takes it away and presents me with a couple of crutches. I have to learn to walk again, again, and any time anyone washes a floor – which, in a hospital, is a lot – the crutches spin out from under me and dump me on my arse. My arse can cope with that – but my pinned together leg cannot.

I sulk a while and sit in my bed. Physio-sadist Jill says, grand. Stay put. Makes it so much easier for me to find you when I have some agony to inflict...

I get back on my sticks, and treating those little yellow 'Wet Floor' signs with the respect I now understand they deserve, I pick my way about the place.

Altogether there are twelve floors. Most of them with names I can't hold in my head let alone pronounce. A&E I know from Sky Living. Radiology is where they take me to see how many bits my leg is in, ICU is intensive care, HDU is high dependency, basically intensive care lite: floor 11, obstetrics and gynaecology – remains a mystery for many years to come.

I sneak down into the basement, the floors where patients aren't welcome. I say sneak – no one's sneaky on crutches. But the fact that it takes me so much bloody effort to get anywhere means that people assume I must have a good reason for being where I am and – apart from holding the odd door open –

they leave me be. I creep along the low lit corridors, I find kitchens, storerooms, maintenance depots, generator bays –

– I wobble and stagger through the whole place.

I have never seen anything like it.

Doctors, nurses, porters, cleaners, healthcare technicians, nutrition specialists, all bustling about their business, all the different things they do fitting together –

And all for one reason.

To stop us hurting.

This place, these people, they take us in and they put us right. Whoever we are.

Even scum they scrape off the road like me, who should be dead.

And they fix me. They fix me so I'm less broken than I was, even before those cunts ran me down.

Last time I see Jill the physio-sadist I say, I'm gonna to remember you, you evil bitch.

Jill says, I'll've forgotten you before the doors swing shut behind me.

Leans in, kisses me on the forehead.

And the doors swing shut behind her. And she's on to fixing the next one.

I go back to school.

They can't believe it. Nor can I really.

I say Mr Harris, I'm going to need your help.

Mr Harris says: how exactly d'you think I can help you, Davey?

I say, I want to be a doctor, Mr Harris. What'm I gonna need for that?

And he smiles, and he's looking for the little hint in my face that'll give him permission to turn his smile into a laugh.

He doesn't find it.

He says you are kidding me, aren't you son?

I say no Mr Harris no I'm not. I want to become a doctor, so I can put people right.

We sit down at his computer. It says 'Becoming a doctor isn't an easy option. It takes years of study and hard work. But as you learn the skills you need, you'll also learn a lot about yourself.'

I say no problem but what's that in terms of exams exactly?

So we look it up on the site. And Mr Harris says, you know Davey, you've not done well enough to be put in for these exams normally. But if you're serious, we could make an exception.

Please do, Mr Harris, please do that cos I am.

He says you'd have to drop back a year and start again.

I say yeah, no problem, that's what I want. To start again.

And he looks at me and says you know what? I have always had a feeling about you Davey, that you would turn it all around. In spite of everything.

So I start again in September. And it is hard. All this physics and chemistry and biology it's like – you know when you're playing on a game and you don't know the controls so you're just pressing things randomly to see if anything works? Like that. I'm writing things and I haven't got a clue what I'm even trying to say.

And the end of the term Mr Harris says you know what is amazing is, I thought you'd stick it maybe a week and then disappear. But you have never given up, Davey. Never once. And I think that is really something to be proud of.

I say thank you Mr Harris I try my best.

He says I know you do Davey. But I think what we have to look at now, is what you're achieving. And even trying hard as you can, you're not doing very well. I don't think there's any chance you're going to get these exams.

And we always talk about not giving up but sometimes giving up is the right thing to do.

I'm at a bit of a loss then.

I lose – a few years.

There are a few years where my life goes as you'd've expected it, if you'd seen me at fifteen, stealing bikes from seven year olds. Or at twelve, ending a decent teacher's career.

But the thing with life is, if you're lucky, it goes on.

I reach a point where I clean up a bit and a friend has a spare room and says, this is your last chance, so don't let me down. Just don't.

I go to the library, I'm looking on the computer for jobs. And most of what's going is stuff I don't even know what it is and then – there's a job at the hospital.

They need a porter.

It's just pushing people around in wheelchairs and on trollies. You don't need any exams for that – and I haven't got any exams. I couldn't be fitter for the position.

When the lady says, so could you tell us why you're interested in this job, I have a lot to say. And I get from the way she looks up from her papers and puts down her pencil, that not many people do have much to say, when they're asked what is their passion for pushing people round on trollies all day.

When I've finished telling her about the hospital and why I want to be part of it, she's quiet for a moment.

Then she says, well if you'll pardon my French, that is bloody brilliant.

So then I'm a porter. I go into this place. I have hours. I have a uniform. I have duties. I get paid.

Everyone acts like it's completely normal.

And I do alright. Cos loads of the other porters act like they hate their jobs.

I love mine.

But then I start to get in trouble cos I chat to people and see they've got fresh water to drink and then I end up not being where I need to on time.

One of the sisters takes me aside.

Says it's all very well making nice with patients but if they're not getting to theatre when they should that's time wasted and money wasted and that's no good for anyone.

She says maybe giving you this job, maybe we made a mistake.

I say, no, no you didn't, I'll chat less I promise, please, please –

She says no you've got me wrong. I mean, maybe you should get more involved with the patients, if that's what you like doing.

There's a job as a health care assistant going. Which is like feeding people, getting them dressed, washing them, taking them to toilet. And on her say so, I get it.

And I'm properly part of the team now. I'm wiping arses but I'm also taking pulses, monitoring respiration. And fuck it – arses need wiping! We'd all want our arses wiped for us, if we couldn't do it ourselves.

I work my way up, I get a few certificates that mean they can give me more responsibility. And one Thursday morning, we're talking about me going to part-time so I can study for a diploma and register as a proper nurse –

And they wheel in this stinking clutch of limbs, curled up on a trolley.

I know him straight off, though I haven't seen him for years.

My dad.

ALAN
I'm looking down

The edge of the blade pressing in

To the hint of flab round his gut.

And the waxy skin.

The hair in the belly button like a thousand trampled daddy-long-legs.

Foul.

And perfect.

Someone loved that belly once.

Because someone loved all of him

The way you do with kids; you love them

Even as they're shitting all over you.

And that love is everything

And then somehow you wander away from it –

PAUL
He crumples to the floor.

And for a while I just lie there cos it seems very much like he's in charge of this situation but

He's not. Of course he's not.

He's just crying.

And getting myself back together I realise he's done a really shit job of tying me up.

I realise I can grab the cord with the fingers of my right hand and pull

My left wrist out.

So I do.

And I'm lying there –

He's still bloody crying.

There's this spanner, at his side.

And I have played thousands of hours of the most violent games there are

And yet I have never, ever really hit anyone, in real life.

Almost as if there's no fucking link at all, between things that are pretend, and things that are real.

But here I am now.

This guy has broken into my flat.

Attacked me.

Would've killed me but for his basic being a pussy.

And inches from my hand a weapon that *he* brought into the situation.

If only I have the nerve to grab it.

But do I? Actually do I?

It turns out yes I do.

And he turns and looks up at me.

Confused.

And then – his expression turning to rage at the unfairness of cold hard events and

I have never hit anyone

But right here and now anyone would say, I'm allowed to hit this fucker.

And I bring the spanner down on his head.

And a second time.

And a third.

And he slides to the ground.

And then I just kind of roar over him, like this –

PAUL roars.

And then I hit him once in his guts cos

It feels fucking amazing.

ALAN
I couldn't ruin that foul, perfect belly.

Because once something's ruined, it's ruined..

You never get to go back

To when it wasn't.

PAUL
– I go for a piss.

I go to my gleaming downlit marble bathroom

With power shower, plunge bath and

With WiFi speakers to pump sound from my music provider and 4K TV

And I stand there do a great big piss out my semi-erect cock.

While the man that tried kill me lies bleeding on the lounge floor.

And then I call the police. Tell them

I've just physically overpowered an intruder who broke in to my flat.

They might wanna come clear up the mess.

ALAN

In court they ask me do I have anything to say. I say

Though I failed my son. I failed to pay Paul Thompson back for what he's done

This has to stop.

I hope whenever a son or daughter suffers

Cos of some piece of sickness dressed up as art

There'll be a mum or dad, mad with grief

Who will find the scum responsible and

Pay them back what they are owed.

I hope from this day on, every film director or game maker or so called artist will have to think

Whatever horror they put into the world

Might be played out on their own bodies.

Because powerful people get rich pumping filth into our lives

And ordinary folk must do whatever it takes, to keep our children safe.

And I see the reporters and correspondents and bloggers

Writing and recording my words. Putting them out into the world where

Social media and algorithm-driven websites will spew them

Over and over again, never letting them be forgotten –

– and it will only take one. One person to hear, and see

The rightness of what I'm saying

One person with nothing left to lose,

To do what I couldn't. Go out and get revenge.

One person and then –

– we have a movement.

The judge listens. Takes a sip of sparkling water.

Rules that I should be hospitalised in a secure unit

For my protection, and the protection of others

Until I no longer represent a threat to the public.

PAUL
Walking out of court, I text my dad, tell him the verdict.

Dad never texts back.

I announce the trauma of nearly getting my guts cut open
means I no longer feel safe in my own country. And so with
great regret, I decide to relocate our entire operation to the
States. Where the tax situation has recently become highly
advantageous.

DAVEY
Still three sugars?
Dad? Still three sugars in your tea?

ALAN
Still? It never was.

DAVEY
I'm sure I remember / you having –

ALAN
'Member that dog? What was her name?

DAVEY
Maisie.

ALAN
Maisie. You look after her?

DAVEY
Did my best.

ALAN
Course you did. You spoil her?

DAVEY
What's spoiling a dog?

ALAN
You let her sleep on your bed?

DAVEY
Yeah.

ALAN
You backed into a corner while she's all legs in every direction?

DAVEY
… Yeah.

ALAN
You spoiled her.
You might as well. They're not with you long.

DAVEY
There'd been a fire, in his flat. Fallen asleep with a fag hanging out his mouth.

They'd brought him in for smoke inhalation.

ALAN
Can you get me a fag?

DAVEY
Last thing you need.

ALAN
Is you being a cunt.
So how'm I doing?

DAVEY
What do they tell you?

ALAN
All sorts. I don't trust 'em.

DAVEY
Well you know you breathed in smoke.

ALAN
That'll happen, if you're in a fire.

DAVEY
And that gave you problems breathing.
But it seems like that was just aggravating what they call an underlying condition.
D'you get out of breath, like if you run for a bus?

ALAN
I haven't run for a bus since the seventies.

DAVEY
If you walk upstairs.

ALAN
I live in a ground floor bedsit.

DAVEY
Have they talked to you about emphysema?

ALAN
The word might have been mentioned.

DAVEY
Dad, it means your lungs are collapsing. This is serious.

ALAN
How long?

DAVEY
What d'you mean?

ALAN
How long before'm better?

DAVEY
What've they said?

ALAN
Weeks, a month, what?

DAVEY
What've they said?

ALAN
I'm asking *you.*

DAVEY
In your notes.
It says, you've been told it's a question of managing your
condition.

ALAN
Okay.

DAVEY
D'you know what that means?
Do you?
Dad?

ALAN
Will you help me up, son. I doubt I'm allowed that fag in here.
(Beat.)
Bit of a fucking relief.

DAVEY
Relief? How would that be?

ALAN
I wouldn't want to go, you know. Demented. Feel myself
slipping away.

PAUL
And after a year or two when I'm settled, I decide to move my
father to the States. To be closer to me.

That's quite a distressing process.

I explain it as carefully as I can, but his Alzheimer's is fairly
advanced by this stage. So he doesn't know what's happening
to him or why.

He fights the orderlies trying to get him on the plane.

They have to restrain him.

Secure him in his seat.

Sedate him for the journey.

It's the bewilderment, I think, that's worse. Maybe worse than the terror.

In the States he gets the best treatment my money can buy. The clinic that's treating him has a dementia research fund. I donate large sums. Not to save my father – of course – but in the hope that others won't have to suffer.

As he undoubtedly does.

Dad stops eating. The clinic warn me without nutrition he won't last long. I do some reading and learn it is possible to fit a tube into the stomach and feed him artificially. The consultant's not keen. He says, is it of benefit to your father to prolong his life at this stage? Might it not be kinder to let nature take its course…

And I say,

I want my dad with me. I want my dad with me and I don't care what it takes. So if you're not comfortable taking my research grants, I'll find another clinic that is.

They fit the tube. Nature does not get to take its course. Because I don't permit it.

DAVEY
When the hospital kicks you out, you could always stay at mine.

ALAN
Kind of you. I won't impose.

DAVEY
Where'll you go?
You need to look after yourself.

ALAN
So people tell me. I'll be fine.

DAVEY
You will bloody not be.

ALAN
I can hardly put you over my knee, but I'm still your father.
Less of the backchat, if you please.

DAVEY
When he's due to be discharged, I make sure I'm on shift.
Help him pack, take him down to reception.
I wheel him up to the door. The cold isn't a chill, it's a full fist
in the face.

ALAN
See you then, son.

DAVEY
I haul him up, hand him his crutches.

There's a covered path down to the bus stop.

He doesn't get half way. Stops against the wall; reaches out for
the back of a bench, lowers himself down.

The door opens before me. Frozen air scorches my chest,
Christ knows what it's doing to his. I stand beside him.

D'you need a hand?

He doesn't look up.

You're gonna miss the bus.

He doesn't look up.

I'll get the car, shall I?

Dad?

He doesn't look up.

But his head sags.

Surrender.

PAUL

I sit with Dad an hour. There's no sign he knows I'm there.

I prop his head up, and he rasps.

I take his shrivelled hand in mine

And I squeeze it, as hard as I can.

I crush his wasted fingers in my fist –

– and he squeezes back.

And his fingers like wires, cut into me.

And I have to fight to pull myself free.

I prise open his eyelids.

I peer in.

There's no rage or fight or spark.

But he's there. Trapped there.

Alone. In the dark.

DAVEY

I remember when I moved into my flat being pissed off there was only a shitty single bed.

Turned out a blessing. I moved the sofa into my bedroom, put the shitty single bed into the kitchen-cum-living room, and put Dad in that. So he had the telly and I could chat to him when I was making dinner and stuff.

I got him oxygen tanks, made sure he took all his inhalers.

I looked after him the seven weeks until he died.

I kept thinking there might be some big conversation. Say when he'd had a drink.

But he was short of breath. It was difficult for him to talk.

But leaving – that came easy enough. The old bugger never changed.

I'd been home an hour.

Given him a bed bath, so he was all spruced up.

We had the telly on, I was in the kitchen making tea.

Macaroni cheese, except I didn't stretch to a sauce I just boiled the pasta, buried it in grated cheddar and slid it under the grill.

He wasn't eating much by then but when I had something he liked a taste.

I turned to rinse a plate in the sink and realised he wasn't moving.

I dried my hands, walked over, felt his neck for a pulse.

Nothing.

The stubble on his cheeks, the creases round his eyes, the burst veins in his nose – all there, just like they ever were.

But I was alone.

Again.

ALAN
At the secure facility where I am held, the chaplain says

You've got years ahead of you, in this place.

People turn to drink, to drugs, to get them through.

Let me tell you, those things might seem to help,

But they only make it harder.

I say, no, no I'll not be touching them.

He says I'm glad to hear that. But they're not the only crutches people depend on.

There are other things.

There is, blame.

There is blaming other people for what we have done ourselves.

And isn't that what you're doing, Alan?

Blaming the man who made this game

Instead of facing your own guilt?

And I say to the chaplain

I know how a priest gets this sort of duty, pal.

Because there's nowhere else will take him.

So you fuck yourself, you kiddie-fiddling bastard.

And what keeps me going, are memories.

Memories of my son. Like –

Bouncing him on the bed.

He loved it. Just bouncing, up and down.

That was all it took. Me bouncing him.

And him crying out,

Duh, duh, duh, duh.

Cause he couldn't say Dad properly then.

And I was gone before he learned.

DAVEY
When my dad went he was clean, and warm, he had company, and his supper was on the way.

I did that for him.

ALAN
And that's the thing. The memories run out.

Cos I was only there with him for – barely eighteen months.

I play and replay them, as long as I can

And in the end

They wear thin.

DAVEY
I did more for that bastard, than he ever did for me.

Because I am ten times the man he was.

PAUL
Once Dad's gone, it's –

We've got a lot of good people in the company, I find my job is

Saying yes or no to ideas rather than coming up with them myself and

Turns out I can get that done quick – yes, no, yes, yes –

And that's me for the day.

Two of the design team fall in love. Get up the duff.

Look into the legalities and realise the cheapest thing is

To get married. At the wedding, she pats her belly, says

You know what you need?

I do not.

You need

Something that's more than you are.

Something to overwhelm you.

So I adopt. A ten year old boy.

And he overwhelms me.

His name's Ethan. First time we meet I say, bit of a hawk, are you

He says nothing cos he's got no clue.

I get through the trials, the interviews and

They tell me I can be Ethan's forever family.

I bring him home and –

I'm on high alert every single second. I'm so exhausted

He goes off to school, I'm falling asleep middle of the day

All the books say give it time don't have expectations and I

Respect expert advice of course but

He's hugging me, calling me daddy from day one and

I'm not, you know? I'm not. He's just saying it, it's

Pure survival instinct, means nothing,

And I feel nothing

Except exhaustion, and worry

And then

After maybe – six months?

It's like all the anxiety crystallises into something else

And I can just begin to see how that something else would
become –

Then one afternoon my driver phones to say he's at school
and Ethan's gone.

And the school say Ethan was supposed to go home with his
friend.

He had a note.

Ethan's not answering I look him up on find-my-phone

But he's switched off.

And I thought I knew what worry was

But I did not. I had no clue.

I learn what worry is that night

Over three hours until

My phone goes. And

It's the doorman. Downstairs.

Ethan's just walked in.

Whistling, apparently.

He's in the lift on his way up –

He walks in heads straight for the fridge

I can't even speak. He says, what?

What?

I just walked home, with my friend.

That's nothing.

I say but I have a driver, your friend

Can come in the car –

Ethan says, Daddy I want to walk, I tell him

Mate, the streets aren't safe

He laughs. I'm going out of my mind and

He's laughing.

Says Daddy everyone walks the streets. Everyone.

And I talk for a long time and

Finally I get through, he starts to understand, he promises

Hugs me

Tells me he loves me.

The next week does it again.

And again.

And on Friday doesn't come back at all.

Messages me says he's staying with his old friends

With his cousins, from back home,

But then his phone's off.

I've got my driver my PA me everyone looking

And I think I should call the police but then

A kid that looks like Ethan does

If he runs.

If they see the phone in his hand and decide

It's not a phone...

Every siren my heart stops

Every news report of anything, I feel sick

I sweat through three shirts I shout

At everyone who comes near me and

If anything should happen to him –

He comes back Saturday like it's nothing.

I say, it's a bad neighbourhood, it's not safe

He says it's my neighbourhood Daddy.

It's home.

And I say okay then

Okay.

And when he goes to school Monday

I have my PA phone the adoption agency I tell her

Whatever it costs

Whatever

Make this go away.

ALAN

But I made Davey once.

And so I make him again.

Every night, I pull the blanket over me.

I drift down towards sleep but then –

There.

There.

It starts

With him, gurgling in the room next to me.

That gurgle he makes when he first wakes up.

The gurgle that will work its way into a cry.

And I lie there, eyes closed, hardly breathing.

Her next to me.

And him next door.

Feet away. So near.

And each night, I give him a life.

I pass the hours, dreaming every detail.

I start with his boyhood, school days,

The facts as far as I know them and then

I have to make him. Again. And again.

And every night his life works out different.

Every night his life is hard

But every night, my Davey turns it all around.

In spite of everything.

Every night he turns out to be

Ten times the man I am.

And the pride in him. And the love. The hot, choking glow of it,

In my chest, my shoulders, my throat,

So long as I stay, in that bed, not moving a muscle –

DAVEY
Fifteen. Walking home.

I turn a corner, and a stupid seven year old crashes into me

On her stupid seven year old's bike. Ribbons and flags and

Little diamonds threaded through the spokes.

I grab the handlebars, hold tight. Her dad jogs up.

Sorry mate, sorry 'bout that you alright?

Birthday girl's a bit wobbly on her new bike.

– girl hops off, wraps herself round daddy's leg –

You're alright though, aren't you?

Dad's a little bit more than twice my age. Greasy hair, grey trackie bottoms over black shoes.

Girl's a little bit less than half. Her bike might be new, but her top, her jeans, her trainers are not.

I say – no. I am not alright.

And dad looks at me.

Sees what's in my eyes.

And I know the muscle at the root of his cock has gone loose and

The muscle at the base of his arse has gone tight

And all he wants to do is turn and run

From the vicious little shit I've become

But he's stuck. Cos of his stupid kid. And I say

You know what might make things alright? I never had

A bike's nice as this. What if I take it, go for a little ride.

And dad says, come on mate. Please.

The girl's saying daddy, I don't want him to take my bike.

She's on the edge now. He says it's okay baby,

The man's just messing about. Just a joke. He's not gonna.

And he looks at me.

And he's basically begging me.

And I get called kid or shit all the time, but I never get called

Man, and him –

His hand finds its place at the top of her head, she looks up

And the smile he forces into his eyes,

And the smiles that answers it from hers.

the smile that says everything's alright.

I never saw a smile like that.

ALAN
Every night, I dream the man he might've become

If I'd been there to hold the boy's hand.

And it's enough. For me.

DAVEY
And how is that fair?

I can't bear it.

I can't bear to let that smile be.

So I rip the bike from her,

Push off, speed away into the night

The stars

Unreachable above me.

THE END.